C000174559

By the same author

Poems
Cages
To See the Matter Clearly
The Region's Violence
Twenty One Poems
Another Full Moon
Sibyls and Others
Climates
Fifteen to Infinity

Play
All Citizens are Soldiers
(translation from Lope de Vega)
– with Alan Sillitoe

Stories
Daylife and Nightlife

Selected Poems

Ruth Fainlight

HUTCHINSON

London   Auckland   Melbourne   Johannesburg

First published in 1987 by Hutchinson Ltd,
an imprint of Century Hutchinson, Brookmount House,
62–65 Chandos Place, London WC2N 4NW

Century Hutchinson Australia Pty Ltd
PO Box 496, 16–22 Church Street, Hawthorn,
Victoria 3122, Australia

Century Hutchinson New Zealand Limited
PO Box 40–086, Glenfield, Auckland 10, New Zealand

Century Hutchinson South Africa (Pty) Ltd
PO Box 337, Bergvlei, 2012 South Africa

Photset by Rowland Phototypesetting Ltd
Bury St Edmunds, Suffolk
Printed and bound in Great Britain by
Anchor Brendon Ltd, Tiptree, Essex

ISBN 0 09 171081 2

Acknowledgements are due to all the periodicals in which these
poems – sometimes in different versions – first appeared.

Contents

Equinox

More than a week of storms,
Storms and sickness,
Has stood between now and my last clear view of the moon.

In two more nights she'll be full.
Thunder, bruised clouds, a sea like melted stone,
Confirm her waxing arrogance.

Full moons had no such heralds through the summer,
Nights of stars, moon discreet
Somewhere in all that glitter. Now the stars have no chance.

This is her season of power, she is everywhere.
The wind scoops mock moons,
White crescents of waves on the violent water.

Three times magnified, she flashes through streaming cloud
Like a wrecker's beacon.
Her lurid halo makes the sky seem hollow.

Time is slowed down by storms: more will happen
Before she gains full circle
Than between one full moon and the next in calm weather.

The Angels

They're poised like statues, civil, dignified,
Interested even, as photos on tombstones are
By a stranger who peers curiously.
The soil is stony, friable. Dry roots break
As I clutch out to stop my downward slide
Into the pit, the place they're solemnly
Admiring. Why don't I cry for help? They seem
So courteous. One would surely bend
From his shallow ledge, reach out a hand.
But my tongue stays still as the empty sky,
As their faces in the stern unwavering light.

The Infanticide

I left my baby there among the trees,
Rain-rusted leaves, decayed stalks,
Twigs husked with grey and white moss.
The black mulch makes a soft bed.
Perhaps he will not cry, lulled
Till I am far enough away by sky's dazzle,
The touch of ferns and air.
From the top of the wood I hear nothing.
Silence is like a plastic sheet
Over his stretched mouth, stifling
His thin alarm, powerless to stop the mist.
I left my baby there among the trees
And now the frogs can have their will of me.

Dawn Chorus

There comes a moment when the tide turns;
Light has won again. The birds stop singing
For a long moment, then begin again
On a more casual note. They've done it:
Dragged back day, tipped cool light
Over the lock of dawn with the nervous force
Of their throats. Some strength of mine
Was sapped to bring that toneless even glare
And settle the question: after each dawn's
Struggle, in the clear white of exhaustion,
Insomniacs float down wide canals of sleep.

The Spirit Moving on the Face of the Waters

At first it seems to flow forward.
But sea's as rooted as a wheatfield,
Slides from crest to trough forever,
Heaves its shining mass
But never throws the rider.

Suspended in the bowl of continents,
Ocean dreams of margin,
Nirvana of dissolution,
Spray flung onto stone,
The heavenly beaches of evaporation.

Waves goad the water
With the shape of freedom.

To See the Matter Clearly

Through reason's telescope the figures
Seem distinct and small.
A jeweller's precision must have
Formed the cunning limbs, instilled
The counterfeit of feeling that
Articulates those manikins.
Their piping voices barely reach
The ear, and eye is strained by such
Elaborate enamelling,
The play of each expressive feature.
It's easy, though, to change the focus,
Be overwhelmed by giant agony:
Huge soft pitted faces mouthing
Pain, and clumsy yearning gestures.
Shift glass again, turn down the sound,
Retreat to that high vantage point
And leave them thrashing in the undergrowth
That through the telescope
Shines beautiful as jewels.

Sleep-learning

All that I try to save him from
Is what he dreams about.
I watch his face
Each night emerging clearer,
Stern son who reads my dreams:
The dreams I had
And those my brother had
And which my parents learned from theirs,
Moving behind mauve lids
That seal his eyes.

He dreams I want to leave him,
Roams through night forests, desolate.
And I dream I've abandoned him:
Pleasure and atonement.
Next morning both our faces
Mark the change:
Mine with the guilty look of those
Who knowingly succumb to dreams,
And his the gaze
Of someone learning.

Lilith

Lilith, Adam's first companion,
Assumed her equality.
For this she was banished.

God had created her
From the same earth as Adam.
She stood her ground, amazed
By the idea of differences.

Adam and God were embarrassed,
Humiliated. It was true –
They had been formed
At the same time, the two
Halves of His reflection.

Her expectations
Should have seemed justified.
But Adam needed to understand God.
A creature must now worship him,
Constrained and resentful
As he was. God encouraged him.

To guard His mystery, God
Made Adam swoon.
There, when he awoke,
Awaited Eve, the chattel.

Eyes downcast, his phallus
The first thing she noticed.
The snake reminded her of it.

That nagging ache in his side
Where the rib was extracted
(In memory of which
The soldier thrust his spear)
Keeps Adam irritable.

Lilith's disgrace thus defined
Good and evil. She would be
Outside, the feared, the alien,
Hungry and dangerous.
His seed and Eve's fruit
At hazard from her rage.

Good wives wear amulets
Against her, to protect themselves.
Lilith is jealous.

Fire-queen

Unseen, snow slides from over-laden boughs.
Spume of flakes, flurry of light, cold smoke;
Kaleidoscope of crystal and lead and flame.
Then silence again as it sinks,
Weightless, lost, white into whiteness, down
To permafrost encasing molten turbulence.

That core answers the sun-spots, flares
When her impotence most torments – she,
With her presumptions, her gestures, who has chosen
This place rather than any other
To expose herself to the gnawing ulcer
Of her own true nature. Such is her kingdom,

Fire-queen of the absolute north,
Who rules by satire, inertia, disdain;
Touch blunted to ice, ears sealed,
Sight gone, reflection congealed, mirror
Shattered aeons ago, rather than see
Merely a pattern of line and colour, flat

As the diagram of what a face might be –
Which to recognize would mean to accept
The clamour of voices, imploring, complaining,
But silent, that rise from her brain like steam
From a tubful of churning laundry.
But silent. Her thoughts – unspoken, ignored.

Their heat is the power that freezes, motor
Of her repression-machine, refrigerator
Of frightful patience, rigid mastodon throne,
Sealed and invisible ice-pyramid,
Red-hot iron maiden of self-hatred
She's trapped inside by refusing to listen.

Screams settle like snow and never thaw.
Branches petrified under their burden
Of murdered desires. She sits like Lot's wife,
Ambitionless as death, perfect, absorbed
Forever by her silent incantation,
Beyond the need for sanction, or praise.

snow poem

      birds stream over the houses opposite
I watch from my window
      one veers, passes through glass as if it were smoke
settles on my table

      it is snowing
      I stare at whirling flakes with such intensity
they drift into the room
transform it to a paperweight

      snow covers my papers
      the bird prints patterns with his feet
hieroglyphs appropriating
what I've written

      the bird flies up   one flake
approaches, huge, revealing
its precision and its symmetry
before it muffles me

Silence

When you ask for consolation
From one of them, burnt children
Who were never loved – or so
The explanation runs –
They do not understand. Perhaps,
Like speech, it is a skill which must
Be learned at its specific
Moment. Once past, nothing
Yet known can activate
That latent aptitude.
The child remains both deaf and dumb;
The one you turned toward –
A loud, gesticulating mute.

How they torment, who always
Must retreat, as if attacked
By such demands, whose last defence
Becomes exposure of a pain
They moan and rage is fiercer far
Than yours. Heart-broken, you muffle
Your own complaint, adjusting
To the region's violence,
Leaving grief abused, unspoken –
Until, beyond the reefs
Of hopelessness, nothing seems lacking
In this solitude. You've grown
Accustomed to the silence.

Pigeons at Villa Belmonte

After he mounted her, wings fluttering
With joy of domination,
Neck iridescent with coppery
Lombardy green and the terra-
Cotta of the Villa Belmonte
(She smaller, darker, reserved, the same
Grey surrounding the shutters)
She strutted onto his neck, as if
In casual imitation; hopped off,
Then up and down, across, a few more times.
They bent their heads towards each other, seemed
Affectionate, their burbling cry conjugal.

I've read that pigeons, caged and left,
Will pluck each other bare and bleeding,
That they're more murderous
Than wolves, with no inborn restraint,
No code for peace which might allow
Retreat or dignified surrender.
Strange choice of symbol used
For love and tenderness, and yet,
Because they're beautiful, they serve.

Two Blue Dresses

What I should wear outweighs
Almost every speculation,
As if clothes could disguise.
A method to evade other
Uncertainties, and yet
The details of a costume
Recollected serve to fix
The character of past events.

The era of that blue silk dress –
Totally different from
The year I fell in love, revived
My aunt's old cashmere blue.
Its bias cut and open-work,
That silver buckle-clasp
Low on the hip, enchanted me,
Though out of fashion then.
The very fact became supporting.
I felt a heroine,
And just as well, those first weeks
Of my first, unfortunate,
Short-lived affair. The stylish frock,
Eleventh-birthday gift,
All ruched, had skirt and sleeves puffed out.

I can remember how
I stood and posed before the glass
Entranced, and half afraid
To see reflected in my eyes
The probability
Of loneliness, but more, the wish
For all that came to pass.
I recognized the destiny
I still attempt to grasp.
I nerved myself to welcome it.

That moment, proud in finery,
Has seared my memory
More deeply than the tears I shed
In cashmere, in despair –
The end and the commencement
Of my girlhood, two
Shop-window mannequins
Who almost seem alive.

God's Language

Angels have no memory,
God's language no grammar.
He speaks continually,
All words variations
Of his name, the world a web
Of names, each consonant
Proclaims a further meaning;
The unacceptable
Also the true, beyond
Time's bondage. Thus angels
Forget all contradictions,
Accepting every statement
As a commentary.
Their purpose is to gaze
Upon God's works, and listen,
Until the day that he
Pronounce the name: Messiah.

Velasquez's *Christ in the House of Martha and Mary*

You stare out of the picture, not at me.
Your sad, resentful gaze is fixed on what
Is only seen reflected in the mirror
On the wall behind your shoulder, perspective
Through an archway cut from sandy slabs of stone
The same warm brown from which you wove your bodice.
That old servant by your side is whispering
Admonitions and consolation – her
Country wisdom. But your attention lapses
From those words of resignation as much
As from the pestle lax within your hand,
The plate of fish, white eggs and pewter spoon,
Wrinkled chilli and broken garlic cloves
Strewn across the table: this, your world,
Precise, material – all you yearn to leave,
Though fear and duty hold you. You cannot find
Courage for the negligence of faith
To justify a gesture similar
And so what right to join your sister there?

My Grandparents

Museums serve as my grandparents' house.
They are my heritage – but Europe's spoils,
Curios from furthest isles,
Barely compensate the fact
That all were dead before I was alive.

Through these high, dust-free halls, where
Temperature, humidity, access,
Are regulated, I walk at ease.
It is my family's house, and I
Safe and protected as a favoured child.

Variety does not exhaust me.
Each object witness to its own
Survival. The work endures beyond
Its history. Such proof supports me.
I do not tire of family treasures.

Because no one remembers who they were,
Obscure existences of which I am
The final product, I merit
Exhibition here, the museum's prize,
Memorial to their legend.

The Field

The field is trampled over utterly.
No hidden corner remains unchurned.
Unusable henceforth for pasture:
Sheep and cattle must feed elsewhere.

The field was torn by battle, dull
Explosions, trenches dug for shelter,
Vehicles which wheeled, reversed,
Hunted down the last resistance.

The field is strewn with bones and metal.
Earth which had not felt the air
During millennia, is now revealed
To every element and influence.

The undersoil surprises by its richness.
In battle's lull, at night, the farmer crawls
To estimate what might be salvaged
Of his lone field's potentiality.

If he survives, the field holds promise
Of great abundance, a yield astonishing,
Unprecedented as all he hopes for.
The field is fertile. He must survive.

A Fairy Story

The princess in the fairy story
Discovered that a happy ending
Had unexpected consequences.
The castle in the wood concealed
A certain chamber. Her knight revealed
A taste for flagellation. And when
He tired of protests and capitulation,
He rode away – until another kingdom,
Dragon, maiden who could not be won
By any simpler method, was stumbled on.

He then would stay, enter the lists.
He loved the risk, the praise, that combat
Or the guessing game where death
Remained the final forfeit. He loved
A distraught princess, never could resist.
Their fear attracted, their wavering spirit.

Once upon a time, their taming was
The reason for his quest, but now exhaustion,
Boredom, made him pleased his dragon-
Surrogate could test them first.
If they survived the monster's ardent breath
That smoky taint made them delicious.

The rescued princesses compared
Sad stories, boasted of their sufferings,
Exaggerating the ordeal.
They dressed each others' hair, changed
Robes and jewels, waited impatiently
To see the girl who next would join them.

One day, outside the crumbling walls
Of some obscure and unimportant
Principality, the knight was bested.
The dragon fled, dragging bruised coils
Through hedges, across muddy plough-land.
The princess would not follow him,
But turned her back and went inside the town.
The watchers were not more nonplussed.

The knight rode home, sent messages
To all his friends. They drank and sang,
Tortured his wives – it was an orgy.
Next day he bade farewell to each
Blood-brother, each noble companion,
Vowed the remaining years to penance
Somewhere far from this vile shambles.

But first, before he set off with his squire
Down that faint narrow path which lured
Deep into the misty forest,
A splendid tomb must be constructed:
Memorial to those princesses,
Obedient victims of his destiny.
The monument still stands, although
The castle fell to ruins long ago.
The knight died on a battlefield.
Their legend: fatalistic, gory,
Fit matter for a fairy story.

Grace-notes

My solemn simplicities, my vows,
My protestations. Tum-te-tum.
Self-accusations. I don't know how
To free myself, to overcome.
Except sometimes, a bird or a tree,
The light on the marsh – direct,
Without equivocation – speak
Of a power that seeks no effect
Outside itself, existing purely,
For which there are no synonyms.
It's a zone I approach unsurely,
That harsh place – where no hymning
Can drown the weak, explaining voice,
Nor grace-notes disguise the wrong choice.

Vertical

Who told me my place?
It takes generations
To breed such a true believer.
It needed centuries,
Millennia, to produce
Someone who instinctively knew
The only movement possible
Was up or down. No space
For me on the earth's surface.
Horizontal equates with delusive
When only the vertical
Remains open to my use
And influence. But
I am released by language,
I escape through speech,
Which has no dimensions,
Demands no local habitation
Or allegiance, which sets me free
From definition:
Jew, poet, woman.

The Lace-wing

Does the lace-wing see me? I stare
Into its pinpoint ruby eyes, head on,
At its bristly mouthparts, my nose brushing antennae.

When I look away the lace-wing turns
Abruptly, as if dismissed or freed.
Its shoulder-pivot swings a thread-leg forward.
It moves briskly across my paper,
Then disappears under a corner.

The intensity of our mutual
Examination exhausted me.
We almost exchanged identities.
Our pupils throbbed with the same shared
Awe, acknowledgement, and curiosity.
We met beyond confine of size or species.

Next day, the lace-wing still is here.
It clings to the window-frame, drinking
Sunlight. It survives for its moment.
And what sustains our two existences
Remains as much a mystery as God.

Dinner-table Conversation

I began to describe that female connivance
With the man who is duping you: amusement
That overrules outrage and even self-protection –
Like recognizing an art-form, appreciating
A fine performance, evaluating this
Particular one's potential for damage;
Altogether forgetting it's you who will be
The material worked on, yourself who'll get hurt.

Women who feel such things, the man at my right side
Told me (after he questioned me closely
To make sure I meant it, knew what I was saying)
Women who know these truths must accept
The role of Muse and its hampering duties.
I sensed more than a touch of malice
In his assurance. It became a dismissal,
An accusation, a judgement – no praise or glory.

But what I had been trying to explain, and not
Succeeding – he having very good reasons
For refusing to listen – was how awareness
Of this split is exactly the fault-line on which
I must build my own San Francisco: the place
Where hazard reigns and poetry begins.
Would I be more a poet or less a woman
Ignoring past joys and defeats?

He would never surrender his right to be hurt:
He needed a Muse to hate. It's the aspect of play
In my rage that disconcerts. He could not even
Admit we shared a common dream.
I filled my glass. We shall soon be forced
Into the mud, consumed by the same worm.
Till then, I can be as easily pleased by a man
As by the moon, a tree, a child, or my dessert.

The Boat

Who is that person I see   distant   so busy
on the opposite shore   I should join her
she's waiting
a winter tree with scratching twigs
that won't let the wind be its master
she looks like me
but I'm drifting away   slipping   a boat
from its mooring   out   to the centre of the lake
where I'll float and sleep and dream
a black boat
in the heavy colourless silence   empty
simple   with no purpose   while light
withdraws below the water's surface
and the mountains concentrate themselves
fold into their centres
numbed with cold   lulled by monotony
the black boat plunges through the one
sliver of red left   blood in mercury
from the already set sun
last trace of memory
to be eased away by water
before vanishing

Last Days

for B.S.J.

The confirmed suicide, calm and relaxed,
Reassures sometime-anxious friends.

They hope he's recovered, and he breathes deep
Like one escaped from the evil wood, from the need
To fight off every comer.

There the festooning snakes, fierce creatures
He wrestled with between clustering roots
And choking vines, now are flaccid
As cloth toys, punctured balloons, deflated tyres.
But Laocoön and his two sons together
Were never so assailed.

Like a firm machete cut, that gasping, joyous thrust
Through to the meadow of death.

He's there already. No need to hurry.
The decision made, he can linger a while
On the grass, in the sunshine. Nothing will hurt him.

Only that bruised fist of cloud, still
Almost hidden below the horizon,
That abrupt-rising flock of cawing birds,
The rusty lichen marking the eastern direction
Flaring suddenly into their vision
So the hedges seem wounded,
And one hot gust of wind, indicate
The lull before the storm's destruction.

August Full Moon

Whichever I choose to look out from, here in my study,
Where the desk is placed in a corner between two windows,
I see her, the August full moon. Labouring towards
This completion, since yesterday she has freed herself,
Purged and dissolved the humours distorting her shape,
Making her swollen and clumsy, darkened from yellow
Of faded leather into the streaked, mottled red of
An old woman's cheek. As if she had discharged her poisons
Into my veins, today I was almost demented,
Sodden, confused, barely awake or able to move
About the house and garden. But the moon, silver
In a starless sky, windless night after a day
Of stasis and sunshine, is disdainful of such effects
On whoever is weak enough to suffer this draining
Connexion to her necessities: I, who sit yawning
And trembling in spite of the heat of a perfect evening,
Who will soon go, defeated, to bed, to escape
Beyond dreams into emptiness from this moment
When the universe combines in haughty balance
And self-sufficiency to reject me, to wait
Until all the spheres lurch forward one notch and leave space
Again for an opening that hope and change might stream through.

Another Full Moon

Another full moon. I knew without checking
The date or the almanac. Again
I am tearful, uncertain, subdued, and oppressed.
It becomes more an abasement each time
To acknowledge I still respond,
Anachronistic as an astrolabe,
Reliable as litmus paper.
No hope of escape, though I should much
Prefer not to be absolutely
In thrall to the rhythm of ocean and cosmos,
So solemnly primitive, such
A mantic pauper. With her roughened tongue,
The moon curdles my milk of human kindness.
Her maniac yellow eye glares
Through the curtains and follows every movement.
Her purpose is obscure, random, and cruel.
It is worse than being a prisoner, because
Between her appearances I forget
How she rules me, how her gauntleted hand crushes
The back of my neck, forcing me lower,
Making me grovel, ridiculous
And awful as a manticore.
I wonder if this is the only way possible,
If it must be true that there will never be space
For wit or humour in the universe
We share, and for all my days I shall bear
The scars of her torture, marked forever
As her creature and her fool.

The Other

Whatever I find if I search will be wrong.
I must wait: sternest trial of all, to contain myself,
Sit passive, receptive, and patient, empty
Of every demand and desire, until
That other, that being I never would have found
Though I spent my whole life in the quest, will step
Clear of the shadows, approach like a wild, awkward child.

And this will be the longest task: to attend,
To open myself. To still my energy
Is harder than to use it in any cause.
Yet surely she will only be revealed
By pushing against the grain of my ardent nature
That always yearns for choice. I feel it painful
And strong as a birth in which there is no pause.

I must hold myself back from every lure of action
To let her come closer, a wary smile on her face,
One arm lifted: to greet me or ward off attack –
I cannot decipher that uncertain gesture.
I must even control the pace of my breath
Until she has drawn her circle near enough
To capture the note of her faint reedy voice.

And then as in dreams, when a language unspoken
Since times before childhood is recalled (when
I was as timid as she, my forgotten sister –
Her presence my completion and reward),
I begin to understand, in fragments, the message
She waited so long to deliver. Loving her I shall learn
My own secret at last from the words of her song.

The Demonstration

Of course I'd throw my children from the sleigh:
Last, frantic bid to gain time. If only
The wolves hold off a while longer.
If only the horses are strong enough.
We race across the steppe,
The sky behind as dark as a Palekh box,
And the wolves' mouths red as inside the box.
When will their hunger be sated?
Are there enough children? Better, perhaps,
Not to survive such exposure of lust
To remain alive at any cost.

Nothing too precious or sacred to sacrifice.
I'll tell you all my secrets in desperation –
Secrets I drag into the gaudy light and betray
To evade the question to guard my privacy
(Such is the style of my conversation)
If only you'll leave me alone.

I'll slip from my coat, leave my skin between your hands
Like a moulting snake. I'll breed another family
And feed the wolves again, and veer and dart
Back past the ermine spoor across the snow
To match your questions against my frankness,
To the place where you are waiting:

Where my bones will be broken and hammered and ground
And carbonized, and that black powder strewn
Over the bloody residue.
And then we'll rise, re-made, re-vivified,
Intact – my children and I – and the wolves
At the runners, whose hot breath fouls the sleigh
Where my children and I prepare another demonstration.

Hair

We with the curly hair belong
To ocean, those whose tresses lie
Close to the skull, fall straight, are claimed
By all sweet waters, brooks and rivers.
Thus for our crown.

               But body's growth
Affirms the spiral: torso and
Limbs attired in robe of such fine-
Woven mesh of undulation,
Whether conch-coiled or sparse as down.

The salty powers control. Dew-pools
And clouds submit at last to tides.
The moon throws shadows on your face
But glints triumphant on the three
Places that always taste of sea:
Looking into whose waves we drown.

Pompeian Dreams

That lamp of pale brass,
Roughly shaped and finished,
Wick twisted from goats' wool
Pulled off the fence
Where it clung to the wire,
Filled with the olives' last pressing
Too rancid for anything else,
Its cone of smoky flame
Sullenly burning. Even
Through sleep, the vapours
Trouble our nostrils.

We're resting on couches
In the stiff, ungainly postures
Of corpses caught by the lava.
And outside the house,
Which stands near the edge of the cliffs,
Dim moonlight and vague
Shudders of summer lightning,
Hiss of the hidden sea,
Seem part of the dream:
A noontime darkened
By ashy eruption.

The whine of a Vespa,
Moan as its motor shifts gear,
Echoes through glinting
Labyrinths, the ocean's
Inner ear: another
Sound-effect to add
To the rush and stamping of bulls,
The droning of insects,
And those muffled prayers and screams
That force their way into
Our dull Pompeian dreams.

My Position in the History of the Twentieth Century

Strange, how I've never lacked a certain confidence,
Been so dissatisfied with my face and body
That I couldn't cheer myself by posing at a mirror
Sucking my cheeks in and raising my eyebrows disdainfully.
Small, trim, not especially sturdy or slender,
Large-chested (though small-breasted) rather,
It's a source of comfort to study the disparities
Between fineness and toughness, my own special markings.
I am not troubled because most people are taller.
Eyes always meet on the same level.

Lucky to live where it was not dangerous
To look like me (no need for a yellow star).
My good fortune took me far from the Holocaust –
Though it's easy to imagine how it feels
To read those scrawls on the station platform wall,
To be the African from whose shocked, sick face
I had to turn away when I sensed how he hated me
Watching his pain, knowing we both knew
He could not pretend those words did not stigmatize.
His appearance as much his expression and pride
As mine is – but I can believe that white skin is not
Yet a primary signal to trigger hostility.

What I'm describing is privilege: the actual physical
State of one who expects and depends on such luxuries
As acknowledgement (my self-confidence never
Subjected to a real test), who has not felt anonymous,
Stripped down to hopelessness, numbered and docketed, trapped
In gross, alien, inexpressive matter, until
The only desire left was for the magic formula
To make me vanish. I flaunt my being manifest
To whoever wishes to read the signs,
And what seemed most private and unique in me
I find dependent on my place and time.

(1972)

Moon

Moon, like a bruised rose-petal
Sinking into a small pool, like
A disk of metal, pendant
Of a Saxon necklace, fragile,
Almost corroded through
By time and soil's acids,
Earth's ceaseless tiny shifts
And movements. Moon, I look at you
And think of Japanese prints,
Of mist and sad, cloistered ladies.
Moon, floating over the marshes
Like a fine slice of Prague ham,
Tender, pink, nearly translucent –
Oh, angelic gluttony!
Old reliable Moon, who
Always makes me write poetry.
My sister Moon.

A Sibyl

Her eyes have an indrawn look,
like a bird hatching its eggs.
To whose voice is she listening?
Anxious, the questioners, waiting
those words, but she seems relaxed
and calm, turning the leaves
of her book, does not even
glance down before her finger
points the message: this cave
familiar as a nest,
and she, its rightful tenant –
no longer forced to make
a choice between two worlds.

Aeneas' Meeting with the Sibyl

Hunched over rustling leaves spread out
before her on the stony ground, like a skinny
gypsy with a joint dripping ash in the corner of her mouth
quizzing the Tarot cards, pulling the shabby
shawl closer round elbows and shoulders, then squinting
shrewdly sideways up at a nervous client,
the Sibyl greeted Aeneas. 'Don't tell it from them,'
he pleaded. She was sitting cross-legged, right at the door
of her cave, and he'd heard how often the wind (Apollo!
he thought, it's draughty here, no wonder she looks
so pinched and cold) shuffled the leaves into total
confusion, which she didn't seem to notice or
amend. 'Don't show them to me. Say it in words.'

'You're all the same,' she grumbled. 'Always wanting
more than you pay for. Of course' – tilting her head
sideways on that mole-strewn stringy neck
(he saw white hairs among the dusty curls)
an inappropriate cajoling smile
distorting her archaic features – 'if you give me
something extra,' she wheedled, 'I'll do you a special.'
The tattered russet-purple layers of skin
and cloth wrapped around her body dispersed
an ancient odour of sweat or incense as her movements
stirred them. Through a hole in the skirt he glimpsed a lean
and sinewy thigh, and feet bound up in rags.
'Come inside, young man,' she ordered. 'We'll be private there.'

Remembering what came next: his search for the golden
bough, their descent into Hades, the twittering shades,
his painful meeting with Dido, the Sibyl's answer
to Palinurus, and then, at last, embracing
Anchises his father, and learning the destiny
of their descendants, the future of Rome,
Aeneas found it hard to reconcile
his first impressions with the awesome figure
who led him safely through the realm of death
and to the daylight world again. He looked
back from the shore to where she crouched outside
her cave, waiting for another questioner,
and saw she had assumed the same disguise.

The Cumaean Sibyl   I

She was the one who, three by three,
burned her books of prophecy
when the asking price would not be met.
Like a wise old nurse who knows that children
rage and fret, but when night comes
creep back into her arms, she watched
the flames, abstracted, stern, and calm.

Her face seemed veiled, the net of lines
a mask, a zone of darker air,
penumbra of another atmosphere –
as though she stood before a fire
deep in her cave, brooding upon
time past and still to come, far from
this splendour and destruction.

Tarquinius Superbus gasped
and broke the silence. 'I'll pay your price.
More than my nurse or mother, Sibyl,
is your worth to me, your prophecies
and wisdom.' 'The same price as for all
the nine.' 'Agreed.' She raised her hand,
the fire died, the last three books were saved.

The Cumaean Sibyl   II

Because she forgot to ask for youth
when Apollo gave her as many years
as grains of dust in her hand, this sibyl
personifies old age: and yet
those withered breasts can still let down
celestial milk to one who craves
redemption: a dry tree, not a green,
the emblem of salvation.

The Hebrew Sibyl

I who was driven mad and cast out
from the high walls of Syrian Babylon
I who announced the fire of God's anger
who prophesy to those about to die
divine riddles
am still God's oracle.

Mortals in Hellas will claim me
name me as from another city of birth –
Erythrae – one of the shameless.
Others will say I had an unknown father
and my mother was Circe
brand me a crazy impostor.

But when all has taken place
when the walls collapse and the Tower crumbles –
that coming time, when knowledge is lost
and men no longer understand each other –
no one will call me insane
but God's great sibyl.

Sibyl of the Waters

Noah's daughter
sibyl of the waters

first sibyl
the most ancient

with Shem, Ham, and Japhet
saw her father naked

already she had prophesied
the flood

and understood
it was the nakedness of God.

Arms raised in invocation
officiating at the altar

where the Ark had grated
upon Ararat

she placed the burning brands
shielding her face

then crushed the dove to death
against her breast.

The Delphic Sibyl

The tripod, the laurel leaves, the robe and style
of a virgin, though I was an honest widow of fifty:
because of my sober gaze and my docility,
the elders of Delphi chose me and taught me
what had to be done with the tripod and laurel leaves.
They offered a drink from the holy stream, showed me
the cleft in the rock where I must sit and breathe
mephitic fumes and chew the leaves until
my head began to swim and words came blurred.
Those gentlemen of Delphi's best, most ancient
families, our city's noble priests,
quite overwhelmed me. I was a simple woman,
obedient, eager to please, and honoured
by the role. And even had I wanted to,
been bribed to do, there was no chance
to slant the auguries. Petitioners
would proffer written questions first to them,
and their interpretations of my drugged
and mumbled ravings were determined by
Apollo's demands and the city's political needs.
I was an ideal oracle, they told me.
Thus I grew old, though monthly more confused,
appalled, exhausted, and in every way
the opposite of all I once assumed.

Destruction of a Sibyl

Right from the start, the Pythia was depressed.
Every omen came unfavourable.
He'd been on duty at the sanctuary
and afterwards, telling his friend Plutarch
about the catastrophe, Nicander, one
of the priests at Delphi, could still remember her screams.

She'd gone into the proper trance, but how
reluctantly; at once began to speak
in a strange, hoarse voice. Whatever dumb and evil
spirit had possessed her would not reveal
its origin. No curse the priests pronounced
could banish it, protect her or themselves.

Like a ship on a stormy sea, foundering,
when bales of precious cargo are jettisoned
and the galley-slaves pull harder and faster because
of the lash, though their oars have splintered, she lurched
and shuddered, struggling to escape; tried to crawl
on bleeding hands and knees toward the door.

That cowardice could never be purged. No matter
how long they lived, the whole College of Priests
would not forget the shame. Everyone fled.
Contagion of fear: panic alone had ruled.
Apollo's priests abandoned their oracle,
and when they returned, found her broken and changed.

Python uncoiled himself, in all the glistening
length of his body, come back to remind them of
the ancient goddess, the Mother Apollo usurped.
It was She who had spoken and claimed the soul
of the Pythia to serve at Her altar and be
Her oracle forever in the underworld.

The Cimmerian Sibyl

These habits come from the old place,
customs brought from home: almost
the only memories of endless
trees, a northern waste of cold
and dark beyond the Caucasus.

Because it was always so, here
on the shores of the Hellespont I still
must have my drum and lance, the three
mushrooms and sacred feathers, before
I rise to heaven and touch the stars.

Everything I know was taught
by the last sibyl able to
recall those days. Crippled, toothless,
and blind, she told me tales of how
we fled the Scythians, and ravaged Thrace.

I learned the steps of the magic dance
(my body burned in trance, the music's
beat made me gulp gallons of water
to quench such thirst) got by heart
the words that trap the reluctant god.

He slides under my skin as smoothly
as the blade of a knife in the hand of one
who slits the pelt and pours warm blood
from the throat of a perfect sacrifice.
Does god or sibyl then pronounce?

But now we are too near Greece, and priests
interpret my oracles, move
between me and the god, stifle my power,
altering the ritual;
fearful; changing the old ways.

Hallucinating Sibyl

As though burning upwards,
her waxy flesh become
candle to the flame of Apollo,
entirely possessed,
sibyl of Thrace,
sister of Pythagoras,
hallucinating sibyl.

Flakes of snow swirl and
drift through the cave mouth.
Eddies of wind
intensify the glow.
The brands throb
like the heart still beating between
the split ribcage of the sacrifice.

Entranced before the fire,
open-mouthed, throat and chest
reflecting light like a breast-plate,
naked shoulders shadowed
and glinting eyes rolled white
to see armies clashing,
phalanxes in the heavens

above the roof of the cave:
her mantic vision penetrates
through rocks, earth, roots
of winter-stripped trees,
the turbulent heavy sky
that shrouds the land
from the Euxine sea to the Hellespont.

Further back, beyond
the circle of light, the influence
of its noisome, pungent
fumes, stand priests
with the dagger and bowl for the blood
she drinks, the skins to clothe her
after she has prophesied.

Candle to the flame of Apollo,
entirely possessed,
sibyl of Thrace,
sister of Pythagoras,
sibyl hallucinating –
but not yet begun
to use Apollo's words or speak with his voice.

Sibyl on the Run

Vague gaze from tired grey eyes
under the wide brim of her hat,
the fine-grained white skin of her face
mud-splashed, hair tangled, uncurling,

harried by wind and rain, she creeps
through the door of the smoky hut, and quick
as a snake, wary and furtive as
a forest animal, thrusts out
a scratched hand to take one
of the oat-cakes from the hearth, crumbles it
into her mouth, gulping with haste

looks round the silent circle of watchers
(no need to doubt, these were believers)
then reassured, straightens her back,
raises her chin, loosens her ragged cloak,
arrogant and proud; announces
herself: the wisest sibyl on earth.

Sick Sibyl

The ecstasy that drives salmon upstream
to spawn and die, eels across oceans,
seal to their breeding grounds, deer hundreds
of miles north with the wolves who follow
to pick them off, geese winging south,
insects into fatal nuptial
flight, all united by
the spasm that verifies existence –
the ecstasy I never once
have felt: my ecstasy entirely
different, my ecstasy
a self-consuming sickness, an envy
of my questioners, who are one
with everything that lives and feels –
sustained, embraced, and blinded by
the shimmering haze which only my
sick eyes can pierce to see the truth,
the future, and the end of love.

Blocked Sibyl

Sullen or stubborn, self-willed,
stupid, or just plain finished
as a sibyl – sometimes it happens
that way: one day, someone
who'd seemed absolutely right
for the job will dry up.
Hair messed, skin blotched, eyes
angrily or hopelessly
averted (but it's easy to tell
she's been crying) she won't answer
even the simple question:
What is it? from her apprentice-attendants,
much less pronounce. Maybe
she's sickened by laurel leaves, smoke
from the brazier, the sweet, foul stench
of anxiety. Better
be blind than always forced
to see those supplicating gestures.
Secretly, they've begun
to appal her – she's afraid that quite
soon she might break down,
laugh or weep with despair
at the most solemn moment. Finished
or freed: she knows as well
as they that she's useless now,
a blocked sibyl.

Rescue of the Sibyl

for Françoise Claustre

After our climb to that distant mountain plateau,
when at last we stood close to the chasm's dangerous edge,
and leaned across the shaky wooden railing
to fathom what lay hidden in its depths,
from that opening rose a smell as harsh as ashes
dowsed with water, a curling vapour dank
and raw as floats above a marshy waste.

An aged creature, her guardian, perhaps,
uncocked his rifle, began his tired patter.
'Those steps lead down to the quaking rocks. In the deepest
cave, our famous sibyl sits on her tripod,
chewing laurel leaves and prophesying.
I am the only one who can interpret
every word she speaks. For a fiver I'll take the lot.'

But we gave him money to go away instead,
and the other two unpacked their sensible macs
and brandy flasks for protection against the damp.
How thoughtless and deprived I felt, as well
as freezing cold. I hadn't prepared myself
at all for the expedition, hadn't even
formulated one serious question.

The sides of the cleft were slick and wet, they curved
away like vertigo. As though peering through torn
drifting cloud from a plane when a current of air clears the curdled
atmosphere, I saw something moving, a horrible
dancing, the stones were revolving, atoms of earth
vibrating and boiling. There were groans and flashes of lightning.
Then the fumes blew back, thicker than before.

The bravest of us moved toward the abyss.
With each rung trod, the turbulence retreated.
She drove it below, a sullen, defeated dragon.
The staircase lay exposed as a flimsy construction
and there, on the mud and grit at the bottom, stood smudge-pots
and clumsy machines to delude any watchers, convince
them the rocks had been quaking. Ashamed, we followed her steps.

That poor wretch, terrorized and abused,
stammered and rolled back her eyes when we finally found her.
It was months since she'd seen daylight or breathed fresh air.
Between her teeth were half-chewed leaves, and her mouth
and chin were stained from their juice. Anxious and trembling,
like a hostage newly released from her ordeal,
she could not believe that rescue had come through a dream.

The Sibyls in Amiens Cathedral

Thin-waisted Gothic sibyls
with pale calm faces
under wimples of clean Flanders linen,
holding your classical
attributes in elegant
fingers: the book,
the palm, the sword, the scroll,
images eaten
away and fading back
into the flaking
painted plaster and stone.

I can just distinguish which
is the Delphic one,
the Libyan, the Cumaean,
though your look and style
are those of later days,
Christian times,
your colours the gold and blue
of chapel banners,
soft madder pinks and reds
of hawthorn flowers,
lush Somme-river green.

Your sister, the Tiburtine,
told Augustus
of Christ's coming, and so,
as oracles
of his triumph, on these cathedral
walls you stand
with the Prophets – proud pagan women,
half forgotten:
like the message you brought once,
but long ago,
to troubled northern souls.

The Libyan Sibyl

She casts away her clothes like soul's ascent
from the world of matter, shining arms upraised,

appears about to move with the ease of a dancer:
a hind setting its feet on the highest place.

Blinded by heavenly light, her eyes are closed.
What need of text – her message a psalm of praise?

It has come, the triumph of love above understanding:
Eternal ardour, ecstasy, and grace.

The Phrygian Sibyl

Speaking the language the first humans spoke
on that mountain plateau, homeland of Kybele,
Great Mother of the Gods, goddess
of caverns and wild beasts – words
only her eunuch-priests now
can understand – always, at the beginning
of spring, when the frenzy of lamentation
and blood-letting has changed to joy at His
rebirth, the Phrygian sibyl, possessed,
blesses the whole earth – rivers,
herds of horses, flowering vines
and lovers – making the oldest promise
in the name of the Mother: eternal life.

The Shinto Sibyl

White snow settles on the sacred peak,
white clouds drift between the cedar boughs,
white bear and antelope, wild boar, run there.
White boulders mark the ever-trodden path.
White the robes the ancient pilgrims wear.
White the sunrise through the eastern door.

Long white hair hung down the sibyl's back,
white flowers from the branches of her crown.
White light reflected by her flashing glass,
white paper fluttered on the stick she bore.
White stone the pavement where the miko* danced,
white drum she beat, and white her moving feet.
White sound I could not understand, her song.
Dead-white, but open-eyed, her face in trance.
White eagle-feathers left upon the shrine.
White bird that cried her message to me: 'Pure'.

*priestess, sibyl

A Young Sibyl

At first she appears
candid and chaste,
yet when she stands
in front of the altar, opens
her mouth, and the voices start
to speak through her throat
in that plangent blare,
everything is changed.
Does she draw down the power
or does the god ride her?

The sanctuary is dark
but her slender form
grows larger, seems
surrounded by a glare,
a holy nimbus.
The odour of stables
is stronger than incense,
and blurring all her phrases,
the snapping of reins
and champing of horses.

Ageless, sacred mare
who gallops unshod,
one of Apollo's steeds,
over past and future.
Those words have meant war.
Blameless though dangerous,
her gnomic sentences
bring secrets back to light,
unriddle old mysteries
and knot new ones.

Introspection of a Sibyl

If only I could be aware of what is happening
in that void, that gap, that murky, fathomless cleft
where space and time must exist
between inspiration and the sound of my own voice:
the truth I never once have heard
a moment earlier than my listeners.

But I am no more conscious of the prophecies
than I can understand the language of birds.
A bird is singing now.
In spite of legend, like everyone else,
I wonder and guess at its message.
My oracles come like birdsong – or how I imagine
they must begin to sing – by instinct,
neither needing nor able to think.

The most terrible phrases burst from my mouth.
My profession is to doom strangers.
Already, as a girl,
playing ball with my friends in the village square
or feeding my tame pigeon, I remember
being more appalled than my parents
by what I'd say: an unforgivable insult
dealt out in all innocence, or a blurted sentence
like a gift to confirm good fortune.

How I admire control, and yearn to achieve it.
I've become almost grateful to those who control me.
Before, I never knew when it would begin.
But the closed, startled expressions
on the faces of those standing round
– as though shutters crashed down –
meant again I'd defined or foretold,
unerringly exposed the poor secret
some old man kept hidden all his life:

with sight as sharp as an eagle
who spots the frightened creature
veering back and forth, exhausted,
across a rocky mountainside,
maddened by the shadow of its wings –
and heavier than every element,
surer than the laws of gravity,
swoops for the kill.

After a few times, you recognize
a universal wariness. It takes longer
to fear yourself, to accept the certainty
of never illuminating that blankness,
that vital hiatus when the demon or angel,
the god, perhaps, takes possession
and you don't exist
yet have the power of a god.

Panic of falling – said to be
the sole inborn fear of a human infant.
Deeper than fear, I've learned, lies the greatest pleasure:
nausea and exhilaration of plummeting free,
the glee of surrender to nullity, temptation
more primal than any craving for security.

And the price for such knowledge? To have
absolutely no command over your life,
your words – no possibility
of calculated effects or tactics or policy.
But how useful you can be to others; and how lucky
if rather than burning or stoning, they protect you,
feed you, and let the simple folk praise you,
keep you safe as a caged bird,
and call you a sibyl.

Only the Magpie

Only the magpie among all its kind
had to be caught for the Ark, and ever since
bear Noah's curse. Yet beyond thought, more
acute than any thought, his rush of pale
and dark against the clouds and shooting twigs
evoke that time before the Fall when just
the wish to fly created wings and skill.

In paradise, fulfilment and desire
were close as white to yolk of an egg. Now,
desire destroyed by its pursuit, the bird of joy
cannot evade the hunter's net. Harsh
chatter of magpies out on the lawn. They pose
sidle and hop, pull worms, lift off, and never
wonder which pinion to use first.

The Route Napoleon

Pollarded trees produce new growth –
this year's twigs and leaves displayed
as evidence. Trees marked by cryptic
streaks of paint, posters, reflector-disks
pressed into their trunks, wounds roughly dressed
with tar. Trees planted to absorb
the fumes of traffic, clothe embankments
and disguise the motorway. Trees
used; trees with the hopeless, doomed
servility of mutilated slaves
or trophy prisoners from some
forgotten war. Trees that can
no longer represent another realm
or further possibility,
but stand there, rooted, by the side
of the road, trapped as much as any
speeding driver or his passenger.

Deadheading the Roses

All day I clip the withered blossoms from the roses,
cut back till where at join of stem and leaf
I sense the chance of one more flower.

I work against maturity and the full cycle,
try to stop the dull hips from ripening
and using that energy

I want to divert towards more buds and flowers,
repeat the same glory, achieve what yet
I know to be impossible:

rejuvenated immortelles; far easier than
to accept the pressure of further growth,
the destiny that hardens petals

into firm, streaked knobs of seed disdaining beauty
for the sake of the future: that power
the artless rose-bush manifests.

Because every rose on the trellis witnesses how
nothing can halt the closing of one phase
or shorten the interval between

fruition and death. While I tear my hands on thorns
in a losing fight against autumn, the same
wind parching the roses' leaves

is driving me nearer to my destination. Only
some miracle could force new flowering,
another scented season.

New Year in England

Red tiles on the village roofs
fusing into a smoky glow
the sun's last fanning rays illuminate.
The marshland and hills.
The further arch of winter blue
above the corded nap of new-ploughed fields.
The floating crimson lake of mist.
The clouds also demand their praise,
those purple banners. Yet something is lacking.

This calm afternoon
of early January, when all the world
still feels as if resting from festival,
needs more lauding, more gratitude,
than the empty road and separate houses,
heraldic television aerials,
the silhouetted tower of the vacant
church, seem able to express.
And I wait hopeful and uncertain
if fit words will come: the glory-song
to satisfy such daunting trust.

With David in the Nimrud Galleries

His first question, after a slow scan
of amazement, was why the crabs, claws uplifted
heraldically between fish and floating horses
with soldiers' corpses tangled in their reins,
incised on the golden limestone tablets, had
too few legs. Further in, we rode behind
Ashurbanipal to the lion-garden
where beasts were released from cages to be shot
(a rich man's safari) and followed with his men
to Marduk's temple to make the sacrifice.
He noted how delicately the shallow streams
of blood from the arrow wounds had been graved down
the lions' sides, like river waves, and pointed out
a gazelle turning to reassure her fawn,
two birds fluttering above a palm.

We talked about the craftsmen who did these carvings.
The columns of captives are endless – how they bind
the composition together. Such strong horizontals:
women, children. One too small to walk
into slavery straddles his father's shoulders.
On another tablet a group of prisoners
have abased themselves. So many battles: Thebes,
Tyre, the Elamite cities. Cunning use
of diagonals – lances, slanting siege ladders.
So many exiles. Centuries later,
these black streaks across a sinewy leg
or fierce helmeted head pitted and stained
by rain and erosion are the only signs left by nomads
who built their meagre fires and sheltered among
jackals and ghosts sharing the ruins of Nimrud.

All Assyria to be imagined
from these fragments. After millennia
of neglect now they are treated as carefully
as premature babies. Each showcase of weapons, vases
or jewellery with its own humidity
and temperature recorder. We felt the hum
of neon-lighting, air-conditioning.
Alone in the gallery as scribes in a library,
I try to tell him what I remember:
confusions of desolation, Mongol invasion,
the waters of Babylon. But he refuses
my sad stories – absorbed and delighted by lion-
friezes, muscled priests with vulture-heads
and taloned feet, banquets and triumphs: the precious
detritus of Nimrud that proves he is immortal.

Childhood

I see it like an illustration in a magazine:
the low and seemly blocks of middle-class apartment buildings,
with half-grown trees and sprinkled lawns between; colours neither
pale nor garish but chosen from the clear, most popular
and tasteful range: grass-green, sky-blue, an undemanding red, and
pointillistic touches from parked cars, fire-hydrants, freshly varnished
doors and window-frames. The streets do not run straight: the land
is hummocky, its dips and curves are on a human scale.

Here on the hill-crest where I stop to contemplate my whole
domain, I feel as powerful and joyful as the wind
that forms the clouds each moment into different shapes.
I wonder at the lives of such exemplary inhabitants,
confirm again that everything's in order, just as it should be
in Toytown; and only then I nod my head and check the straps
and buckles of my skates, let myself go, and swoop down, down,
past houses, families, up the opposite slope and into Heaven.

A Child Crying

Gasps and sobs through the wall from the next flat:
a child's voice in dirge-like complaint whose words
I cannot make out but whose tone accords too well
with my mood – as though it were I in that stranger's room,
bitter and desolate, choked with grief,
oppressed by a world I cannot understand,
that withdraws and refuses to console me.

A child crying. We who can imagine
that to batter the child to silence would be
kinder than to leave it in such distress
(at least would change our own distress), each time
are forced back to that old anguish – hours shut into
a bedroom, crouched behind a slammed door,
stifling in a wardrobe, throbbing temples
pressed against a bathtub; trapped horror
of the cot, suffocating blankets, the sickly
baby colours of their damp itching.

And when at last it has stopped, and the unknown child
is pacified, we are left exhausted and
ashamed as though after torture, capitulation,
and the final loss.

That Smile

Sometimes I find myself looking at children
with that fond soft smile of older women
who've forgotten it all: which made me hate them
when I was yearning for confirmation
of my new maternal status, a decade ago.

But yesterday, though I should have known better
(in spite of those memories) shut into
a carriage on the Northern Line
with a distracted mother and her two small boys,
I felt that same expression blur my features.

Sturdy, rosy, laughing, bundled in anoraks,
pressing their noses flat against the windows,
the naughty children crawled across arm-rests,
gabbled utter nonsense and mixed-up words,
ignoring their mother's restraints and protests.

Truer to their humanity than either
of us, they knew without having to learn
that for the short time given – whether
it ended at Edgware or in seventy years –
the only purpose of living is pleasure.

Maybe the smile that used to disconcert
had a different meaning than I read into it.
Those other women might have been wanting
to reassure and divert me, as I now
tried to catch the mother's furious eye

and make her delight in them, acknowledge
her own two children as emanations
of joy and wisdom; and more than this,
as empty station platforms hurtled past,
I wished that she would smile at me.

It Must

Friends, sisters, are you used to your face in the mirror?
Can you accept or even recognize it?
Don't be angry, answer me frankly, excuse
the question's crudity. I can't – no matter
how often I take the little square of glass
from my bag, or furtively glance into shop-windows,
the face reflected back is always a shock.

Those scars and wrinkles, the clumping of pigment
into moles, spots, faulty warty growths
around hairline and neck, the way skin's texture changes
absolutely, becomes roughened and scaly,
coarse-grained, every pore visible, as though
the magnification were intensified: horrible.
These days, I prefer firmer flesh in close-up.

Younger, I remember how I stared, with a mixture
of attraction, repulsion, and pity, at the cheeks of older
women – the sort I chose for friends. Did they
need me as much as I idealized them?
There seemed something splendid and brave about such raddled
features, crusted and blurred with the same heavy make-up
I've taken to wearing – warpaint, if, as they say,
the real function of warpaint is to bolster
the uncertain warrior's spirit, more than
to undermine and terrify his opponent.

Now, I long to ask my friends these very
questions and compare reactions, blurt out
the taboo words. But we're so polite, so lavish
with compliments, tender, protective – cherishing
the common hurt: tenderness of bruised flesh,
darkness under the eyes from held-back tears,
watery blisters on frost-touched fruit already
decaying, marked by death's irregularities.

Friends, tell me the truth. Do you also
sometimes feel a sudden jaunty indifference,
or even better, extraordinary moments
when you positively welcome the new
face that greets you from the mirror like
a mother – not your own mother, but that other
dream-figure of she-you-always-yearned-for.
Your face, if you try, can become hers. It must.

Divination by Hair

Every few days, looking into the mirror,
I find another dozen hairs turned white.
Though dubious about my purpose, almost
despising myself, I go on pulling them out.
She, the ideal I stubbornly adhere to,
would never search so urgently for their wiry
glint, crane her neck awkwardly
the better to ensure not one escapes
the tweezer; she would disdain pursuit of such
discoveries. White hairs are curlier
and vigorous, age and death becoming
more assertive the closer they approach.

I know it can be nothing but a losing
battle, paltry and ridiculous.
Sooner or later I'll have to choose whether
to be bald or white. I cannot continue
this depilation with impunity.
They'll never grow back as fast as vanity
can raze them. Like one enthralled (it cannot
be mere scrutiny distorts my face)
hours at a time I stand in front of my mirror,
which long before now should have lost its power
and become a superseded altar, not
the secret place of panic, rage, and grief.

I'd prefer to be brave, to let my tresses fade
to mottled grey and white – but even the best
resolutions are hard to keep when every
day's attrition brings a new defeat.
If only it could happen overnight:
one morning I would wake transformed into
that dignified wise matron of my dreams,
matured at last to grace (though I make her sound
like the grandmother on a birthday card –
acquiescent, fatalistic, and
too bland by far – not at all what I mean)
storms calmed, reefs passed, safe harbour now in sight.

ii

Every day, new hairs faded.
Why don't I just accept it?
Why don't I dye it? What difference
would it make if I left them? Age
would not come sooner, nor my actions
avert dissolution and death.
Who do I think I'm fooling?
– No one except myself.
For who cares really whether
my hair is grey, white, or black?
Others, also, are doing their best
to conceal, refuse, forget.

iii

Because death always seemed a mother –
or a grandmother – someone
familiar, now I come near
the time of greying hair, I fear
the mask more than the skull beneath.

iv

Silver hair is the warning sign.
To watch it spread is like catching fire.
I want to smother it, to hide
the mark that shows I'm next in line,
exposed, too near the danger-zone.
I feel death creeping up behind.
Those fading hairs and deepening lines
are the entangling net she throws.

v

Witch from an ancient forest-tale;
goddess; hag; Atropos-Fate;
Kali; crone. Can I placate
you better by carefully hiding the blaze
you sear across my brow, or apeing
your style? Conquering queen, your embrace
is inexorable. Whether I hate
or deny or adore you, you will unmake
me, eternally, and create me again.

vi

days   mirror
          dozen hairs   white
     dubious   purpose
despising
          ideal   stubbornly
                    urgently
                    awkwardly
               not one escapes
                         pursuit
discoveries
     vigorous   age and death
          assertive   approach

                                   losing
battle   paltry   ridiculous
                         choose
     bald or white
               impunity
                         vanity
               enthralled
          scrutiny distorts

                         my mirror
                         lost its power
          a superseded altar
               panic, rage, and grief

               brave   tresses
     mottled grey and white   best
resolutions
          attrition   defeat
                         overnight
                         transformed
     dignified   dreams
               grace
          grandmother
                    fatalistic
     far
          calmed   passed   harbour   in sight

74

Satellite

Light streams into the room:
a presence behind the curtains
pushing against their edges
as palpable
and menacing and volatile as mercury.
Suspended in an empty sky,
above the black backdrop of pines,
that scalding glare,
flattening the lawn into a bald formality.
How could I forget the full moon?

Only this afternoon
impossible to stop the tears
forced from my eyes and down my face:
a water-mask
seen through the beaded curtain of a cataract.
Again and again I'm dragged off-course.
For days I could not wake – tonight,
quite lunatic,
I cannot sleep, but want to go outside, into
that light, and shriek at the moon.

I hope it will end soon.
And yet, if I withdraw beyond
her rule, through cowardice, or
she no longer
focuses her power and ceases to disturb,
how foiled and desolate I'll be:
a barren victory, gained
by banishment
from that world of extremity in which I've lived
as satellite to the moon.

Danger-areas

The landscape, hazed, recedes in layers,
pale heifers munching in the meadows,
hills crowned with castles as in fairy tales.

Those little touches so essential
to create the state of tension
that brings the picture into focus.

It must be strange. Deceptive comforts
of familiarity are not
effectual, are not allowed.

Otherwise, why does he seek
the dragon; why is she, so languid
at the window, hoping for catastrophe.

Romance, that necessary irritant,
becomes the only explanation
of sojourn in such danger-areas.

Again

Suppose the prince who once had been a toad
changed back after a certain span of years.
Perhaps it always was intended.
Happily ever after only meant
a few decades, and this return to earlier
days inexorably programmed into
the experiment. The kindly fairy's
blessing lost its potency as princess
and her golden hero aged together.

Suppose one morning when he woke he felt
the clammy stricture web his toes and fingers,
his mouth begin to stretch into that
recollected lipless grin; and when
she turned to face him from her pillow, saw
in her contracting pupils the reflection
of cold warts and freckles surfacing
like blisters on his muddy skin.
He dared not speak, but waited, numb with dread.

Suppose that night she'd dreamed about the hour
her ball had rolled and splashed into the pool
and that foul toad had hopped towards her, croaked
his arrogant demand, and forced her will.
Yet afterwards, everything was perfect.
As though the time between had vanished, now
she smiled and clung to him, gazed deep into
unaltered eyes. Who could guess the coming
transformation? Let it all begin again.

Animal Tamer

You would have made a good animal tamer –
I can tell by the way you're taming the wild black cat
that appeared last week at the bottom of the garden.
Every morning she comes a little further.
You go outside with a half-filled saucer of milk
and put it down as if you didn't care,
but each day move it an inch nearer the door.

The black cat's glaring eyes have a baffled look.
There's something about you she cannot understand.
You've activated her curiosity.
But still she crouches watchful under the bushes
until you glance away and fuss with your pipe,
and then she dashes across and gulps and laps,
the hair round her neck bristling with suspicion,
peering up at you several times a minute,
relieved yet puzzled by such indifference,
as though she missed the thrill of flight and escape.

Today, for the very first time, you turned and stared
at those yellow, survivor's eyes, and the cat stared back
a moment before she swerved and ran to safety.
But then she stopped, and doubled round and half
gave in, and soon, as I know well, you'll have
that cat, body pressed down on the earth and fur
electrified, stretching her limbs for mercy.

Always Time

There's always time for making love or
writing poetry – the two
activities revealing certain
parallels. Whether those stories
one has often heard are judged
as more amazing or amusing,
it seems no situation's ever
been too complex or unlikely
or ridiculous to stop
determined people.

Words or phrases sometimes come
with that same urgency, and minutes
open up, allow the time
to seize or lure them (whichever method
best achieves your purpose); tease them,
mouth them, use them every way
imagination leads, until
enough has passed between them and
yourself, and you feel sure there'll be
a further meeting.

Then, smoothing her hair and skirt,
straightening his tie, they go back to
their separate lives – return to where
he was before, what she'd been doing;
the prospect of a poem or
an assignation as secure
as such matters ever are –
only the time and place to be
arranged; minds already hard
at work and scheming.

The Function of Tears

The function of tears
must be to serve as language,
a message to others –
yet the bitterest weeping
takes place alone. The message
then for oneself, an urgent
attempt to reach
that shackled prisoner
in the deepest dungeon
far below the level
of the lake.

What do tears express
that words cannot do better?
Tears are the first language;
a glazed face and anguished
moans communicate
rage, pride, regret,
pleasure or frustration,
remorse and hatred:
almost every emotion
sufficiently intense,
before words can be formed.

Each of these feelings
in turn must colour
the soul of the prisoner
abandoned in her corner,
like the shifting greys
tinged by rainbow hues
of light filtered
through tears clogging
her lashes, jagged
prisms of memory
and hope in the gloom.

Such tears have little effect
on the silent warder
who checks the links
of her chain, brings bread
and drinking water
and sometimes even
changes the musty straw.
No one has ever seen
the warder cry –
not his wife or children,
not the torturer.

Perhaps the lake
was hollowed out by tears.
But until the castle
is assailed, besieged,
completely undermined,
with dungeons flooded,
crenellations tumbling,
and torturer, warder,
and prisoner are forced
to shout above the sound
of rushing water,

call to each other for rescue,
swim clear of the ruins,
embrace and cry with relief –
that lake, like the socket
of a giant eye drowned
by unimaginable
grief, will still stare
blindly up toward heaven
and go on weeping,
endlessly replenished
from a fountain of tears.

Fire

Fire, like all servants, must be watched
continually. Fire, the best servant,
therefore the most dangerous. Every
servant dreams to usurp his master, outdo
his arrogance and pomp, his whims, his cruelty.
Servants would create a world
of absolute caprice, a universe moved
by the same murderous totalitarian
ferocity as fire rioting through
tenements, incandescing block after block
of their pattern: a chart lit up to demonstrate
the saturation bombing (those who plot it
being fire's unwitting servants).
Once got loose, fire will eat metal box-cars
and girders, cement structures, papery bark
of eucalyptus trees, household pets or
humans: consume anything. Because nothing
is alien to fire, as the perfect servant
never shows surprise at his ruler's demands
but will supply whatever asked for. Contained,
fire can work miracles, but rampaging
free, reduces even his own hearth
to ashy desolation – then creeps back,
surly, to sit weeping in the ruins.

My Rings

On my right hand since then
I've always worn the ring
my father and I chose
as my twenty-first birthday present.
On my left, these months
since her death, my mother's ring:
the engagement ring he bought her
half a century ago,
and gave to me,
after the funeral.

The only break in his grief,
those first mourning days,
was when he learned
the two of them would lie
together under the same slab.
Ten weeks later, throttled
to death by a cancer, he followed.

If I forget . . . then let
the faded garnet oval
in its antique setting
tighten round that finger
like a garotte; the diamond,
angular, stab sharp
up my arm and pierce my heart.

I spread my hands on the desk.
Prominent tendons and veins
on the back, like hers;
red worn skin of the palm
that chaps and breaks
so easily, inherited
from my father. Even without
the rings, the flesh of my hands
is their memorial.
No need for anything
more formal. Not gold
nor platinum and precious stones
can serve as well
as these two orphaned hands.

Usually Dry-eyed

'Do you cry easily?' At times. Always
at what is called the cheapest sentiment.
Especially when lovers are reunited,
brothers reconciled, son safe and well
at home with his mother, husband and wife
smiling together. Those are the basic tales.

I'm moved to tears also when the hero wins through
and the siege is lifted, the message delivered, the years
of work rewarded – whenever modest virtue
is recognized. They are tears of pleasure
at the closing of the circle, when Heaven sinks
to earth and existence becomes ordered, just, and perfect.

And tears are brought to my eyes by any report
of natural disaster: when rains fail or fish
move away, devastation destroying the labour of hundreds,
sharp-tipped heel crushing the ants' nest.

But tears are not appropriate nor adequate
response to the arrogance of cruelty.
Tears make one impotent. Anger is needed. Anger,
the activist. And anger must stay dry-eyed.

Meat

This subject might be better for a painter,
a moralizing painter – the butcher's window
framing him: anachronistic whiskers,
ruddy face, white coat, striped apron, the sort
of tradesman one had thought no longer could
exist; and her: a proper Chelsea lady
of a certain age, hatted, necklaced,
mackintoshed, whose rouged and powdered cheeks
seem quite another substance than the flesh
of booted girls who stride along the pavement.

The gloomy afternoon accentuates
the disconcerting glitter of the shop:
refrigerator doors, refulgent tiles,
enamel trays displaying cutlets, kidneys,
liver, mince, scallops of veal, oxtails
and stewing steak – that close detail behind which
all the action will take place, and, as
a background (filling in for mountains, say,
or distant vista of a plain or lake)
hang carcasses made ghostly by their sheath
of creamy fat, and ghastly by the blood
congealing in their blackened, swollen veins.

He holds a tray of gobbets out for her
inspection almost deferentially,
as though the relics of a martyrdom,
some tortured part -- and she bends forward, solemn,
thoughtful, curious. Two faces
from the crowd around the rack or headman's block.

I cannot hear, but guess he's vouching for
its authenticity. Each animal
received an individual injection
of adrenalin, to tenderize it
with fear and rage. She's pondering, her vacant
eye reflective as a sphere of gristle,
intent upon deciding what to choose.
And in that chrome and crimson antiseptic
antechamber to the slaughterhouse, they
are the natural focus of the composition.

The New Science of Strong Materials

(With acknowledgements to Professor J. E. Gordon, and the second edition of his book, *The New Science of Strong Materials*, Penguin, 1976.)

Plastic flow or brittle cracking:
whatever the material,
always the inescapable
potentiality within the structure
of either form of fracture:

these two failure mechanisms
are in competition for
all inadequate and earthly matter.
If it yields, the fabric's ductile.
Brittle, if at first it cracks.

Trying to visualize the three-
dimensional reality
of imperfection, dislocation's
vortex, the maelstrom of shearing, I guess
the faultlessness and ease with which

the rows of atoms can reject
the slightest deviation, yet not
acknowledge or accept even
a modicum of individual
involvement or decision.

They barely need do more than shuffle
one small fraction of an Ångström
in position, and quite soon
the incomplete half-sheet of atoms
has been edged outside. The others

have combined, closed ranks. Stresses
and strains, pressure and tension: the language
not only of engineering. Though
the combinations seem almost endless,
the basic elements are few,

their governing rules the same: just different
ways of dealing with dislocation
and stopping fracture, rare
recorded attempts and rumoured
success at cohesion, bonding, and union.

To Somehow Manage a Poem

There's a patched-up, incongruous neatness about his appearance
like a mongol child who's just had his collar buttoned and straightened
and a careless flannel rubbed across his face

Or the photo sent of a hostage, yesterday's newspaper
propped against his chest to prove he's still alive

Or that figure in the witness box, so pale and thin, who whatever
the consequence cannot control his grin –
happy to be out of the cellars, to see
other people after months of one ranting examiner –
though his smile reveals the missing teeth; soon
he'll start to say everything he was told, he'll reiterate

And the hostage's wary muffled voice, scratchily taped,
left at the pre-arranged place, will accuse all his colleagues

And the child will stumble over his age
and name, but somehow manage a poem.

Climates

I. Further . . . Closer

First day of the second half of another year.
Again the evenings will be shorter, mornings later,
the centre of the solar system further away.

This fear of being exiled further from the source,
trapped in the desolation of my own centre,
where frozen winter will be autumn's only harvest.

What could be further than my soul from any centre
of light and warmth and energy? If the sun is a jewel
in its creator's crown, his face is turned away.

But what horror, if he should swerve round and fix his gaze
on me. Nothing I was or thought could endure those eyes
as they came closer, and cauterized my darkest centre.

And yet, I still keep moving closer to the furnace-
centre, that jewelled horror now as cool as water,
where he reigns, lord of all knowledge, where night and day

have the same length, winter and summer eternally stopped
at Heaven's equinoctial centre, closer towards
the promised revelation of his other face.

III. The Distant View

Summer rain
streaming down the windowpane
is the sound of the wind,
and shaking trees,
heavy with their fullest leaves,
are the shape of the wind.

Ten years looking at the same scene,
the same tower, the same steeple.
Either the church is slowly sinking,
or the trees are growing taller.

Always the birdsong. The first
sound at dawn: pigeons
in the chimney, with the changeless message
of another morning.
And only the heaviest rainstorm
can drown for a moment
their mechanical calling.

Flaunting its burden of foliage
every branch and twig moves
in a different direction: thousands
of despairing gestures – an outdated style.
Inside the house, the silence,
except for wind, rain, birds,
makes such extravagant
expressiveness less viable.

Then, between showers, the flat grey sky
is stretched apart, coagulates
to cloud. The horizon returns. The trees
are calmer. Soon the sun will be setting.
Birds begin to celebrate
that blue and crimson certainty.
Everything looks smaller, clearer,
further away, and quickly, before
I lose the distant view and rain
comes down again I close the curtains.

VI. Angel from the North

Now, between July and autumn,
August makes its own season.
The clouds seem higher, piled in sharper
whites and darker greys, the sky
already colder – arctic tones
above the glowing apple trees,
laden with a better crop
than these ten years I've lived here. Next month
such rain would strip the leaves, every
morning raise another ring
of tawny mushrooms, mournful flocks
of martins gathering for their
long journey south. Today, the lawn
shows only greener and more livid
when the storm stops, and still the sun
strikes hot before a further bank
of cloud blots out the light, moving
like an angel from the north –
whose fiery sword of frost will bring
the apples down to rot among
the sodden leaves and faded grass,
and mark the garden like the first-born.

VIII. An Unmarked Ship

An unmarked ship, entering
the harbour of an undefended
town: autumn bears down on the land.
Driven by a north-west wind,
banks of cloud are the weight of sail
carried on its towering masts,

and that relentless grinding back
and forth of harvesting machines
across the fields becomes the distant
shouts for help and last attempts
of the inhabitants to save
themselves before the plundering starts.

IX. Red Sky at Night . . .

Clouds in horizontal bars
lit gold beneath, shaded mauve
above, with flame and scarlet centres.

Puce and dove become a pure
blue sky that deepens, heightens. Red
brick house, red roof-tiles, rose-hips

and crimson autumn leaves. And all of it
my delight, though I am more
one of the hungry flock than a shepherd.

X. Anticipated

This month I've watched the moon through every change
from thinnest crescent into ripeness, from August
languor into clear September. Unseen
between two darknesses, full moon will be
tomorrow morning, just before noon. Tomorrow
night, hours after the unmarked climax,
her strength already waning, will be too late.
Tonight her energies are at their height.

Full moon used to awe me, craze me – now
I feel equal to her power. This
moment perhaps I too have reached an acme,
and the over-arching sky, the garden trees with
their rustlings and shadows, their nightingale-language,
are satellites circling around the centre
everything on earth anticipates
and this one night allows me to become.

XI. To Break this Silence

Wind and trees and birds, this vague and always
changing weather – how they cut me off
from him with whom I share my house and life,
and I am altered by the seasons' power.

Hours each day together. Yet not enough
to counterweigh the glamour I succumb to,
those hours spent staring at the fire. It seems
that nothing happens but the rain and sunset,

night-mist curling through the hedges. The habit
of our mutual isolation forces
me to seek persuasive words to break
this silence – the key and explanation why

the radiance of a sphere of light against
the clouded autumn sky, swathing the moon
like fruit around its stone, confirms that we
have come to be the other's fate and climate.

Passenger

Not watching trains pass and dreaming of when
I would become that traveller, glimpsed
inside the carriage flashing past a watching
dreaming child, but being the passenger

staring out at tall apartment blocks
whose stark forms cut against the setting sun
and bars of livid cloud: balconies crowded
with ladders, boxes, washing, dead pot-plants,

into lighted, steamy windows where women
are cooking and men just home from work, shoes
kicked off and sleeves rolled up, are smoking, stretched
exhausted in their sagging, half-bought chairs,

under viaducts where children busy
with private games and errands wheel and call
like birds at dusk: all that urban glamour
of anonymity which makes me suffer

such nostalgia for a life rejected
and denied, makes me want to leave the train,
walk down the street back to my neighbourhood
of launderettes, newsagents, grocery shops,

become again that watching dreaming girl
and this time live it out – one moment only
was enough before a yawning tunnel-
mouth obscured us both, left her behind.

Here

Here, like a rebel queen
exiled to the borderlands,
the only role I can assume
is Patience, the only gesture,
to fold my hands and smooth
my robe, to be the seemly one,

the only precept, always
to know the truth, even if forced
to silence, never to deny
my unrepentant nature.
I am my own tamer.
This life is the instrument.

And yet the iron hand wears
such a velvet glove,
and dreams and memories
of prelapsarian happiness –
simple actions which, when
first performed, lacked that content –

return to slow my steps
as I climb up and down between
the parlour and the kitchen
to fill my watering-can again
and give the plants their ration,
make me question that self-image.

Some power, created by
an altered vision, moving
to a different rhythm,
annihilates the past, revealing
space enough for another
universe. And there,

where needs and wishes synchronize,
where truth is changed and laws
revised, the capital has fallen
to a friendly tribe,
and I can leave this exile
when I choose, or rule from here.

Stubborn

My Stone-Age self still scorns
attempts to prove us more
than upright animals
whose powerful skeletons
and sinewy muscled limbs
were made to be exhausted
by decades of labour
not subdued by thought,

despises still those dreamers
who forget, poets
who ignore, heroes
who defy mortality
while risking every failure,
spirits unsatisfied
by merely their own
bodily survival.

I know her awful strength.
I know how panic, envy,
self-defence, are mixed
with her tormented rage
because they will deny
her argument that nothing
but the body's pleasure,
use, and comfort, matters.

Guarding her cave and fire
and implements, stubborn
in her ignorance,
deaf to all refutation,
I know she must insist
until the hour of death
she cannot feel the pain
that shapes and haunts me.

Outside the Mansion

As though we stood with noses pressed against the glass
of a window-pane, outside a mansion, dazzled
by the glowing lamps, the music and the circling dancers:

festivity, ceremony, celebration –
all equally alien to my sort of person.
Such a failing passes down the generations.

It could well be a fairy story, half-remembered.
I often wonder if some godmother uninvited
to the party, vengeful, cast her mournful spell.

So profoundly known, the joyless spite spoilers
use to ease self-inflicted pain; envy
and disappointment proudly claim choice of the poison

they gag and choke on. Yet now it comes to seem almost
courageous – I begin to understand how
the warmest most confiding moment must provoke

this inherent disavowal and contempt
of every garland placed to decorate the brow
and hide the eyes before whose gaze we're powerless.

Stronger than the doubt of being right or wrong,
refusal is our sole tradition. We watch
the windows darken as the curtains slide across.

The Prism

Braided like those plaits of multi-
coloured threads my mother kept
in her workbox (beige, flesh, and fawn
for mending stockings, primary tones
to match our playclothes, grey and black
for Daddy's business suits) or Medusa-
coils of telephone wires, vivid
as internal organs exposed in their packed
logic under the pavement, nestling
in the gritty London clay,
associations fray into messages:

codes to unravel, cords to follow
out of prison, poems which make
no concession, but magnify
the truth of every note and colour,
indifferent whether they blind or deafen
or ravish or are ignored; the blueprint
of a shelter against the glare
– and the waterfall to build it near –
the perfect place to sit and hear
that choir of hymning voices, and watch
the prism of the rainbow spray.

Entries

Like notes of music black against the stave,
the look of words and letters in purposeful
groupings, whether printed or written, seems
to convey something more definite
than their overt message, even when understood.

But, thorns on the knotted stems of briars
thick as the hundred-year growth around the sleeping
princess, or a spider-web's decoration
(dried-up flies like November blackberries,
legs contracted in death) how well they hide it.

Dark beetles, swimmers with glistening backs,
etching their hieroglyphs between worm-casts and pebbles,
bird-claw cuneiform and rabbit-tracks
across dawn's snowfall, runic silhouettes
of trees upon the sunset-streaked horizon,
the icicles' oghamic alphabet,

Each mark, spoor, trace, or vestige left,
every shadow that stirs the wheatfield
as if a god strode there, are the imaginings
and melody of energies beyond
control until expressed: entries
in the dictionary of another language.

The Journey

Head against the glass, eyes close
to the train window, everything that grows
along the siding blurs and streaks: a green
and brown and yellow diagram of speed.

Not until I urge my gaze backwards
down the line can I distinguish saplings,
plumy grasses, flowering weeds and briars
sown there haphazard. Lifting my eyes higher,

one pigeon, pale against thunder-clouds,
spot-lit by a fitful summer sun,
rises above a formal wood, dense
trees all the same size, as though planted together.

Softened by the mirror of a tunnel,
my reflected face stared out, much younger,
superimposed like an old photograph.
If I sat opposite, one glance

comparing the two would be enough to inform
myself of every change that time has wrought.
Suddenly, I learned I was not other,
earlier, than what I have become

but only now am forced to recognise.
Wings beating it further up the sky,
to a bird's eye, the whole route is visible.
The nature of the country makes no difference,

nor the hastening traveller's confusion
(journey unended, memories unproved)
between conflicting versions of the legend
uniting images and questions

concerning fate and chance and fortune. Dazzle
of sunlight, then shadow, blinding me in the carriage.
A horse alone in a meadow, the level-crossing.
A steeple. The first houses. The train is stopping.

Launching

Autumn. Early morning.
A bench near the pond in Kensington
Gardens. This park is where
I've watched the seasons change
for twenty years. Under
my feet, yellow and crimson
leaves, colours as pure
as though with death their poisons
were purged; but further away,
against an empty sky,
the rusty foliage
of a shrubbery like a head
of hennaed greying hair.

Through the playground railings
the swings and slide and sandbox
I feared and hated. No one
told me how short such moments
were, nor taught the art
of living in the present.
There seemed so many dream-
scenarios. Now,
the only roles left: leathery
tourist, plastic-bag crazy,
reclusive autodidact, or
admirer of grandchildren's
model racing yachts.

Spring and summer passed,
winter marking its own
bright blaze on what will not
endure, the balance shifts
from hope to human nature,
and the last self manifests,
poised for survival. But meanwhile
come days like this, when nothing
yet seems crucial, blue
and gold and calm, with time
to feed the ducks and learn
the different styles of launching
boats into the water.

After Fifteen
to David

First there were close-ups: fallen petals,
patterned bark, fungus on stones,
a baby's pram – garden scenes.
The playground where, laughing and rosy-
cheeked, you waddled after pigeons
in your padded snow-suit; I,
another discontented mother
by the sandbox. All photographs
which seemed to need between three and six
feet. Then the focus shifted,
lengthened, changed. Now, Sunday
morning in the park, six feet
tall, you stand against the peeling
plane-trunk, look up through its leafless
twigs and branches, camera aimed
at pallid winter clouds. 'Fifteen
to infinity?' you ask, to confirm
the setting. Yes. You have grown
to become the photographer, and time
expands around you like the dizzying
crown of the tree and sky above:
fifteen to infinity.

Love-feast

Sulphur-yellow mushrooms like unlaid, unshelled eggs
inside a chicken's stomach when my mother cleaned it.
This morning, mushrooms on the lawn made me remember.

Bright as dew on the grass and silver with air-bubbles,
a stream of water splashed from the dull brass tap against
the side of the sink and over her red-chilled fingers when she
opened the carcass and laughed to show me how some were almost
ready – yolks only needing their coating of lime and mucus,
while others were still half formed, small as pearls or seeds.

Always, once the chicken was plucked and quartered and boiling,
my mother would take those eggs, marked with twisting coils
of crimson threads like bloodshot eyes, and the liver put aside
on the draining-board in a chipped old china saucer, and fry them
with an onion to make our private treat. In the steamy
kitchen, the two of us would eat, and love each other.

Handbag

My mother's old leather handbag,
crowded with letters she carried
all through the war. The smell
of my mother's handbag: mints
and lipstick and Coty powder.
The look of those letters, softened
and worn at the edges, opened,
read, and refolded so often.
Letters from my father. Odour
of leather and powder, which ever
since then has meant womanliness,
and love, and anguish, and war.

War Time

"Stand here in front of me," my mother said,
and pushed me forward in the downtown office
doorway. "Hide me." Behind my back she fumbled
with a sagging stocking and broken garter.

That garter: salmon-pink elastic crinkled
at the edges, half-perished, stretched too often,
it had lost the rubber button. Her stockings were
always too long. Something else to blame her for.

Her flushed face. My harsh stern eye. Of course
I noticed: the folded rayon top exposed
an inch or two of thigh – soft white flesh,
neglected, puckered with cold. (Another torment.)

Her round felt hat, pierced by a tarnished arrow
glinting in the drafty corner, bent low
as my ten-year-old shoulder, and the safety-pin
held between her lips seemed further off

than that umbrella-tip or those galoshes
of passers too distracted to ignore us.
No peacetime knowledge would assuage the future
we determined, one rainy winter morning.

Or Her Soft Breast

I could not get to sleep last night,
burning on the slow fire
of self-despite,

twisting on the spit that's thrust and
turned in such cruel manner
by my own hand,

until those earthy clinging arms
lifted out of the dark
to hold me fast

and drag me back to the same place
I thought I had escaped,
to see her face

as close as when I knew it first:
smiling, tender, perfect.
My fetters burst,

but the puzzle and the meaning
of my sudden freedom –
her touch on me,

soothing and cool, as though I sank
into a pool and drank
there, thankful –

was it a dream of love or death?
The grave, where I now slept,
or her soft breast?

Lost Drawing

Bare winter trees in silhouette
against a clear cold turquoise sky
just after sunset: during the war,
at my aunt's house in Virginia, I tried
to draw them – trees like these in England
which she never saw – and now,
trees in my garden make me feel
the first true pang of grief since her death.

Between the washtubs and store-cupboards filled
with pickled peaches and grape jam, crouched
into a broken wicker chair,
I peered up through the basement window.
Sketchpad on my lap, with brushes and
bottles of black ink, blue ink, and water,
I wanted to convey the thickness
of their trunks, the mystery
of how a branch puts out a hundred
twigs, the depth and power of evening.

I heard her cross the porch, the kitchen
floorboards creak. As it grew darker,
that halo of light, outlining
all the finest intersections,
faded. Night absorbed the trees
the house the woman and the girl
into itself, kept every aspect
of that time alive, to give
me back today the memory
of my dead aunt and my lost drawing.

The Storm

Harry, I know how much you would have enjoyed it.
I can see your mouth's ironic curve as the heavens
opened. The umbrella over my head was almost
useless – rain and hail at the same slant
as your amused imagined gaze darkened
the side of my coat and trousers. Hard to resist
the thought that while we hurried back to the car
as soon as we could wait it out, cold
and distracted, someone up there was paying attention,
taking notice. The sky had been clear
enough as we drove through the cemetery
gates into those horizontal acres
ignored behind the bonfire sites and toolsheds
of surburban gardens, then parked and walked
between memorial stones to our appointment.
A spare man in a mac held the casket
chest-high as he approached. I stretched
a finger to touch a corner. The brass plate,
engraved with your full name, flashed paler
in the altering light as cloud thickened.

Cut into the piece of ground that was
the grave of both our parents – a square hole,
its soil piled nearby. A superstitious
qualm made me look down: too shallow
to disturb them. It must have been the very
moment the sexton stooped to put your ashes
there – where I hoped you'd want to be:
with them – that the storm broke. Instead of a struggle
with grief, we were fighting the weather, reduced
to the ludicrous; instead of prayer, a dry
shelter was what seemed most important. Water
running across my hands, inside my sleeves,
I took the spade and being chief mourner,
made the first movement to bury you. Harry,
I think you would have found the symbolism
too facile and pompous, and your sense
of humour stopped you taking it seriously,

though certainly delighted by the conceit
of Nature aghast and weeping at your interment,
my poor brother, her true and faithful poet.

In Memoriam H.P.F.

God, the dead, and Donna Elvira
all inhabit the same realm:
the great democracy of Imagination.

Every paradise and underworld
beyond a blue horizon –
Sheol or Elysium –
is a beautiful product of mental function:
conjuration, prayer, and purpose.

I shall not meet my dead again
as I remember them
alive, except in dreams or poems.
Your death was the final proof
I needed to accept that knowledge.

As Though She Were a Sister

As though she were an older or a younger
sister, whom I might bully, flout, ignore
or use, my dealings were not serious
enough. How could I think she was my sister?
What insolence – and luck, to dodge her well-
deserved rebuke. For she, more like a mother
(I the disrespectful child who shouts
and flails and pulls away) till now has not
abandoned or betrayed me. I must have seemed
ridiculous or worse to all who watched,
and most to those who recognized the Muse.

Spring in Ladbroke Square

Embers still coated with ash,
these February buds – while others
already show the glowing nub
of life, each one Dionysus'
cone-tipped staff; and the first raw leaves
unhusked seem frail red curds and fibres
of flesh clinging to the twigs, as though
bacchantes had been here last night
to carry out spring's sacrifice,
and thrown the torn and bloody shreds
of Orpheus' limbs into the branches.

Titian's *Venus and Adonis*

He with that calculating look,
sated, half-rueful, of the local heart-breaker –
mustachioed garage-mechanic – and she,
the blacksmith's wife from further down
the square, mortified yet pleading:
why should he want to leave all
that lavish flesh and golden hair?

Even Cupid is asleep, drugged
by her perfumes and odours, his quiver of arrows
abandoned – but the dogs turn back to their master
and pull at their leashes, as though they sniffed
the waiting boar – and the plume in Adonis's
jaunty cap, stirred by the autumn
wind (perfect hunting weather,
sun pouring through thunder-clouds)
is equally restless. Nothing will thwart him.
Her insistence seems futile, his young
arrogance triumphant, and yet,
her power has never failed before.

Miriam's Well

(from Talmudic sources)

On Sabbath evening, Miriam's Well,
and all its healing miracles –
that holy liquid which for her sake
saved the children of Israel, followed
them through the desert forty years –
moves from well to river, from river
to stream to well.
              After her death,
the flowing rock of Miriam's Well
sank in the sea, to rise again each
Sabbath and work its wonders. Miriam
died by a kiss from God. The Angel
of Death could not take her, nor worms
touch her body. When you draw the bucket
from Miriam's Well, if you want to hear
her prophesy, remember to fill
your mouth with water.

Archive Film Material

At first it seemed a swaying field of flowers
windblown beside a railway track, but then
I saw it was the turning heads of men
unloaded from the cattle trucks at Auschwitz.

Trompe l'Oeil
(at the Villa Farnesina)

A blank niche in a wall
that you walk towards
with a vase in your hand
to place on the painted pedestal.
The pieces of broken glass
the bent stems
and fallen petals
and on the floor a pool of water.
Yourself putting them there.

The Angel

Sometimes the boulder is rolled away,
but I cannot move it when
I want to. An angel must. Shall
I ever see the angel's face,
or will there always only be
that molten glow outlining every
separate hair and feathered quill,
the sudden wind and odour, sunlight,
music, the pain of my bruised shoulders.

Valleys and Mountains

What I know are valleys
between the mountains
have buried beneath them
the crests of other mountains,

and I can see through depths
of stormy ocean
the drowned empires
there before the ocean,

trace the cool fern's pattern
in burning coal,
ancient sunlit
jungles become black coal,

and proving every tale
concerning love's
transforming power,
surely this must be love.

Passions

Let's not mention love. It's like a glowing
stove to someone covered with burns already.
And hate is that dark cave whose depths conceal
a reeking oubliette where rivals groan.
One glimpse enough to turn your head
and make you lose your balance, envy will have you
spiralling from the top of the cliff, down
onto the breakers. Anger is the sea.
Gasping and buffeted, no matter how
you struggle or plead for mercy, you drown. But pride
can clothe those shattered bones with perfect skin,
and breathe into the lover's mouth her song.

Natural History

– then you captured my distracted spirit,
called it down from where it danced and hovered
around our heads, brought me back to myself,
trammelled by your gross and loving grasp,
into the realm of our own natural history,

into that garden where the flowers strain
on bristling stems toward the sun and arch
their petals wider, and the snail's slime-trail
stops at a broken shell as the harsh triumphant
beak stabs over and over through its pulpy heart,

where sounds and smells and colours, taste and touch
of hair and flesh, glistenings, swollen
heats and tension, matter's prodigal
and irresistible excess, all
transform the butterfly into a rutting primate.

The Music

I sit alone in my room
on a cold summer afternoon
upstairs from where you in your room
are playing the gramophone.
Though you don't know it, I open
my own door wide enough
to share the sound of the music.

Another floor up, in the attic,
two adolescent lovers
play a childhood game, just
rediscovered. Laughs, and the rattle
of dice, drift down from above.

Barely more than their age,
hidden on the steps below
the next-door villa, whose stones
still held the heat of day,
my head on your shoulder,
we listened to someone
playing the same tune.

That night, we hurried home
to our new games – perhaps
your memories are the same?
Or else, I have to wonder
why you chose the music.

Death's Love-bite

A slow-motion explosion is what my mouth's become,
front teeth thrusting forward at impossible angles.
Incisors once in satisfactory alignment
cruelly slice through lips and tongue, and molars grind
each other into powder. Though it took almost thirty
years for them to drift so far apart, the pace
accelerates. My mouth contains meteors
and molecules, the splintered bones of mastodons,
galaxies and Magellanic clouds; feels like
a photograph of particles halted in
a cyclotron and magnified a thousand powers,
a microscopic re-enactment of the planet's
coming total fracture, elements dispersing
out in space. That's the truth I clench between
my jaws, behind my face. And all the technical
ingenuity called upon to solve
this dental problem won't heal Death's love-bite.

Calcutta

Carts loaded with sacks and planks
moving into the pre-dawn city.
One man in front between the shafts,
two pushing from the back.

Knees drawn up to the chin,
rickshaw-men asleep
on the poles of their vehicles.
Black crows roosting.

A five a.m. sweeper,
stiff-legged, stooping
at an empty crossing
by the silent kiosks.

The gaunt fronts of hospitals,
their windows bright
as strings of coloured lights cascading
down this wedding pavilion.

And now the hired car goes past
another drug-store, another clinic,
the Panacea Laboratory,
another sweet-shop.

Dark brick obelisks and pyramids
along the ruined paths:
'. . . guide on, young men, the bark
that's freighted with your country's doom,'

Derozio's memorial,
and Rose Aylmer dead
in the Park Street cemetery.
Blood and marigolds at the Kalighat.

Give that girl thirty pice
because she's singing.
But don't look at the lepers'
blunted fingers.

In the Tibetan Restaurant, drinking gin,
middle-class intellectuals
to whom the greatest insult
is to be accused of pity,

and out at Dum Dum airport,
rising above the burning cow-dung pall
that blurs the skyline, another tourist
who can't take any more.

The Power Source

In this part of the country
all through July, sometimes
round the clock, after
the first crop's cut and stacked,
the rape-seed brought inside
that new blue corrugated
plastic barn behind
the churchyard, the driers keep blowing.
Industrial farming. Often
annoying, ignored, it fades into
the background: one more factor
in the ambient pattern of sound.

I can let it lower my guard
and mood – becoming sulky,
agitated – or get me
high on the idea of progress:
a theme to brood on. Either
way, stimulated or
nerve-racked, I find the summer
different than before
I noticed the strain of trying
to be a nature-poet
these unbucolic days.
The power source has shifted.

When it stops, though other
motors seem much louder:
passing tourist traffic,
helicopters spraying,
tractors (drivers earphoned
to muffle their own noise),
the vital note is missing.
I wait its starting-up,
knowing I'll be uneasy
in the interval
between now and the August
combine-harvesters.

The Circle

We did not meet that often: once
or twice a year for drinks, or walking
to the store we'd stop and talk –
she the village dowager,
I the foreigner who'd stayed
a while but then decamped, become
one of the weekend people. Always
I admired that upright stance,
gallant style, and undiminished
presence. She still could play the perfect
hostess: draw me out about
the house, the garden, and the children,
and not touch on the personal.

But the last time – I was crossing
the far orchard, taking a short-cut
to the river – she called me over
to join her and the dogs. I noticed
something different: those fine
eyes never were so bright
before, nor cheeks so gaunt and flushed,
hair disordered, gestures bewildered.
I started to say the usual things
about the weather and crops but
almost peremptorily, was
interrupted and asked, 'Tell me please,
do you enjoy fairy stories?'

It was the end of summer. I
remember watchful apple-pickers
as we paced back and forth between
the trees and she described the pleasure
of rediscovering old tales;
how I wanted to believe
that, like a circle closing,
connexion had been made from past
to present. Months later, a bitter
April day, I hear the news.
The circle was a fairy-ring,
as false as fairy gold, and nurses
guard her from worse bewitchment.

Judgement at Marble Arch

Office girls doing their lunchtime shopping.
Bewildered blond families up from the provinces.
Africans, Arabs, Italians and Spaniards.
Cut-price teeshirts, blue jeans and haversacks.
Oily exhaust fumes and noisy rock music.
Hot August sunshine, then the first autumn shower.

Just past Lyons Corner House,
near Marble Arch underground station,
I heard a low but penetrating moan
by my right shoulder, and turned to confront
a tangle of greying hair not quite concealing
eyes squeezed shut and open mouth (saliva
stretched in threads between the drawn-back lips)
of a woman – about my size and age – wailing
her distress. Her naked goatish legs
in heavy shoes kept stumbling forward,
somehow avoiding all obstructions.
The large red plastic bag in dirty hands
was held as though at any moment she
would cover her head to hide from the assault
of sound and sight, or use it to vomit in.

Someone else had noticed – a caring friend
and wife and mother, I would guess. Our doubtful
glances intersected. Both relieved
from having to make a decision, but wondering
whether – the other a witness – we were committed
to action, as well as pity and horror. Slowly,
through the midday throng, we followed after,
murmuring our uncertainty. Whenever
I got close enough to hear, she was still
mouthing her fear, and curses. The woman with me
seemed as nervous. 'I'm frightened,' I confessed.
'Me too.' Bright brown eyes stared back, grateful.

At Edgware Road a man reached out
to touch her arm. She had become visible.
The circle of watchers broadened. She flinched and dropped,
then stretched the plastic bag across her face
as though it were a magic hood,
the fluttering red wings of a wounded bird,
a shaman's regalia with its tawdry glamour.
'Where's a policeman?' my companion muttered.
I had to get away. 'I'll try to find one.'

In another story I'd take her home and nurse her,
heal her, be a holy martyr.
But I didn't want to;
nor did I want to hand her over.
When I returned from where I'd stood
around the corner in the hotel entrance
the crowd had scattered. 'She crossed the road.' Her voice
had changed – alarmed, perplexed, almost
indignant. 'There might have been an accident!'
'Maybe she's been like this for years,' I mumbled,
ashamed of myself. 'So many sick people
in the cities . . .' 'Perhaps.' For the first time
we had to deal with each other (if we talked longer
might be forced to make a judgement) so said
goodbye, and went back to our separate errands.

The Future

The future is timid and wayward
and wants to be courted, will not
respond to threats or coaxing,
and hears excuses only
when she feels secure.

Doubt, uproar, jeers,
vengeful faces roughened
by angry tears, the harsh
odours of self-importance,
are what alarm her most.

Nothing you do will lure her
from the corner where
she waits like a nun of a closed
order or a gifted young
dancer, altogether

the creature of her vocation,
with those limits and strengths.
Trying to reassure her,
find new alibis
and organize the proof

of your enthralment and
devotion, seems totally useless –
though it teaches how
to calm your spirit, move
beyond the problem's overt

cause and one solution –
until the future, soothed now,
starts to plot another
outcome to the story:
your difficult reward.